# BLACK
# BOOK
# OF
# POEMS

Vincent K. Hunanyan

BLACK BOOK OF POEMS

Copyright © 2018 by Vincent K. Hunanyan

www.vincenthunanyan.com

@vincenthunanyan

ISBN-13: 978-1-7325975-0-1

Also by Vincent K. Hunanyan
*I Wasn't Crying Over You*
*Black Book Of Poems II*

# PREFACE

Dear friend, let me begin this book and thank you for your interest in reading my work. I am very humbled. As a preface to these poems, I would like to say a few words about what poetry means to me.

I believe that good poetry resonates with people on a metaphysical level; you can read a poem without quite being able to put into words why you enjoyed it. It could have been the shivers that ran down your spine or the elevating of your heartbeat. Or, it made you smile, or even cry; made you feel *something*.

A key component of good poetry is honesty; much of the poetry in the world doesn't speak to people because it is forced and pretentious. If what you write is true and honest, and you put some actual effort into it, I believe people will respond to it.

I write only that which *I* know, that which I can feel and try to transcend to the reader through a few lines. Nothing else concerns me.

I think that most people don't read or appreciate poetry because they have been exposed to too much poor poetry, and been told by their professors to interpret them in a certain way, like there is a science to interpreting a poem.

There isn't; poetry, just like any other piece of artistic creation, is subjective. You cannot ruin someone's interpretation of a poem by explaining it. But if the poem doesn't speak for itself, ultimately, it is a failure.

So, please don't ask me what my poems mean, I really couldn't tell you. I can only tell you what they mean to *me*. But by doing so, I would ruin your own interpretation of it.

Whether this turns out to be a work that resonates with you, I have no way of knowing, but I would like to thank a few people, nonetheless.

I would like to first and foremost express my deepest gratitude to my family, who has supported me in all of my endeavors, even when I suggested something so ludicrous as being a writer.

I would also like to thank a few professors from my past; Michelle Huneven and Karen Kevorkian for working with me and pointing me in the right direction, Professor Nersessian for being a great teacher and for introducing me to the world of William Blake, and Professor Torres, for her enthusiasm and passion in teaching English literature.

Lastly, I would like to thank Maggie McGill for inspiring many of these poems.

For best experience, read the poems out loud. Enjoy!

# POEMS

# RAIN

War bells toll, red raindrops fall
Achilles bolts to catch the wind
To clench the rage that lurks within
Spartan soldiers blow their horns
To warn the foe of a gruesome war
And all the while fair Helen groans

Tears up her veins and goes insane
And begs the gods to stop the rain

The Prophet cries *you're all condemned*
And gives his life for a greater end
Simon's Son smiles in despair
And sobs and sighs and plucks his eyes
And lights another cigarette
To comprehend that he is dead

To no result and all in vain
For he forgets about the rain

Dear Dylan sings of times to change
And thousand years go by the same

So Father deems the death of Caine
Yet Caine escapes his frightful fate
And runs astray in a drunken state
To help suppress his dreadful shame

To never be afraid again
And find a shelter from the rain

Another father leaves his home
To be a ------------, rolling stone
And all the children smile in pain
Mother cries and begs and moans
And years go by and all is lost
For the creature cared for most

Is but a picture in their brains
When she went dancing in the rain

The wind grew weak and winced away
And artists came with acts to play
And all were given time to mourn
The distant memories at dawn
The village prayed and children hushed
And all farewells were swiftly rushed

The trees stood tall and insects crawled
And there was no more rain to fall.

## ROMEO'S ELEGY

To broken hearts, to broken dreams
To me and you, to you and me
To all the friends and all the foes,
To those who love and those who don't

To those who have and those without
To parent's scorn, deprived of doubt
To those who give, to those who save
To those afraid, and all the brave

To all the seconds, unforgiving
To the departed and all the living
To those who dare, to those who care
To those in bliss and in despair

To all the smiles and all the laughs,
To all we love, on love's behalf
To all the pain and single cry
To happiness and every high!

## BALLAD OF A BROKEN MAN

Embrace your loneliness; repent,
For all are lonely in the end.
Embrace it, child, and don't let go,
On tales of bliss do not depend.

For in a life of quid pro quo,
Within the current, puppet show,
In solitude you will but cry,
Until your heart can bear no more.

And as your tears fade out and die,
Leaving marks of frail goodbyes,
Bright blue sky will not shed light,
On precious days of sweet July.

The only thing remain will night,
Reveal itself nor wrong nor right.
Sporadically, and out of sight,
Sporadically, and out of sight.

## CITY NIGHTS

In solitude in bed I lie
And all the while the sirens cry
A homeless bastard passes by
The smell of urine rises high
And hides away, above the sky
Forsaken dogs bark in the park
Fireworks in distance spark
And I wake up, and still it's dark.

## BLISSFUL CELEBRATION

The desolate degenerates of cyber generation
Are singing songs in reference to all of God's creations
While popping pills of preference and other medication
And raising spirits of content in blissful celebrations!

## IF I WERE STANDING AT THE GATE

I'd let you in undoubtedly
So you could spread your joy with me
And we would sing and we would swell
As the inevitable farewell
Would slink upon relentlessly
And we would part in grave dismay
And in our graves like statues lay
Until the day, we both await
When we are standing at the gate.

## BRILLIANT MIND

If only I had a brilliant mind
I'd waste away my days, for days
As of this day, I am at waste,
And still I lack a brilliant mind.

## UP IN THE AIR

When I was a child of seven,
I dreamt of God and heaven.
When I was only eight,
I was told to wait.

When later I turned nine,
I saw an act that was divine.
A year passed by and I was ten,
I prayed in pain, he hushed again.

Later still when I was twelve,
I saw a book upon my shelf.
I read it 'till I was thirteen,
As I envisioned fields of green.

Years went by, I turned fifteen;
To become more foul and mean.
By and by, I came of age,
As I reached the final page.

## BUT PERISHED FROM THE EARTH

Fie upon your holy scrolls!
Your bodies burned and turned to mud!
Shame upon your timid souls!
Your kin enslaved, betrayed by blood.
Your voices veiled and damned by birth;
Your bliss, your hopes, your joys, your mirth!
And what is left, my distant friend?
A spot, a piece of sand, your land;
That's all but perished from the earth.

## YESTERDAY

Yesterday I smiled so brightly
Yet you could not help but cry
All the nights must seemed so frightening
When the dark betrays the sky
And the birds begin their screeching
In a dying wish to fly

I truly tried, but couldn't reach you,
For my love for you had died.

## MORE'S THE PITY

More's the pity, youngster
More's the pity, my young friend
Why in cells of rue thy cluster
Until you for your sins repent?

## MY DREAMS
## (WRITTEN FOR THE GUITAR)

I think I'm fine but I'm suppressing;
These feelings, I can't explain.
This play I'm in is quite depressing,
And acting's never been my trade.

Pretentiousness is our foundation,
To hide our weaknesses and pain.
Our eyes reveal our desperation,
And the attention that we crave.

I want to hide and disappear,
For even though I'm not alone;
With hundreds souls inside my home,
I find no inner peace at all.

OUT ALIVE

Hate is easy, love is hard,
You may linger, time will not.
The last string strums; your hours are up,
The time has come to raise your cup,
And bid farewell to all time bought,
The countless lessons never taught,
All the treasures never sought,
And all the battles never fought.

Tick tack, you have arrived,
And no one here gets out alive.

## LULLABY

Little child, why do you cry?
Am I to sing your lullaby?
Am I to stroke your silver hair,
To soothe your soul in your despair?
Am I to hold you to my breast,
Until your sorrows are at rest?

Little child, rest now and smile,
And I'll be with you all the while.
Do not lose heart and cry in fright,
For I will sing all day and night.

## EVOLUTION/REVOLUTION

Bring me closer to the unknown,
We'll live forever; they tyrant's overthrown.
Revolution was our only solution,
Since evolution led to prostitution.

## DRUNKEN DAD

Mommy's in the kitchen crying
Daddy's drunken on champagne
Shattered dreams of futures dying
Children hold their breath again

Mommy's sobbing in contempt;
For every promise never kept.
For all the anger, endless pain;
Things will never be the same.

Daddy beats her like a beast,
Until one day she is deceased,
And the children left bereaved,
Of all the love and care received.

## FORGIVE ME LORD

Forgive me Lord, for I am flawed,
I pity those that pity me.
Suffering torments my heart,
And I grow numb the more I see.

Lay your mines under my feet,
I'll spread my limbs upon your street.
And you can honor my demise,
With tales of truth and other lies.

# I AM

I am the cause of my decay,
I am the end of my desires,
I am the legs that walked this way,
I am the hands, that lit this fire.

I am the mind that thinks I'm fine,
I am the reason that is absurd,
I am the diamond that rarely shines,
I am a sea of empty words.

I am the anger that wants to scream,
I am the pain that wants to cry,
I am the climax of my dreams,
And I will live, and I will die.

## REMEMBER LOVE?

Remember love, how we used to play?
Indulging in day-dreams far away,
While all the singing nightingales,
Would chirp in sync, behind the dales.

Until the sunrise stretched its rays,
On our bare bodies in the day.
And we would smile and laugh and rise,
With happiness inside our eyes.

Remember love, when we used to say,
We'd dance to the second suite one day?

## SHYLOCK'S REVENGE

The villainy you teach, I will execute,
In soft disdain, and silent vile,
I will revenge with but a smile.
And bait your flesh to fish withal;
For all to see your downfall.

Henceforth to stand on top your tomb,
With tears of joy upon your doom.

## ANOTHER CHILD CONCEIVED

My mother bore me in late May,
And I was peeking out the day,
Or the night; she can't recall,
Daddy's sitting home, appalled.
Another child, another pain,
Another mouth to feed, again.

Dad ran away, did not look back,
Perhaps to cut himself some slack.
He couldn't stand the dread received;
Of yet another child, conceived.

## ALL THE CHILDREN RUN AWAY

Parents have forsaken them
And left them in dismay

So the children run astray
To exotic lands to play
To forget the dire past
And to find new bliss and joy
So their smiles can glow and blast

And their hearts pure love employ
And all the time that will have passed
Will soothe their memories, at last
And they will all live happy lives
And have children of their own

A loving husband, loving wife,
And leave all miseries behind.

## INNOCENCE LOST

Your heart is pounding sharp and loud,
Drops of sweat run down your brows.
The blood is rushing down beneath,
You gulp for air, but cannot breathe.

His eyes are dark as depths of hell,
His smile is cruel, and nothing tell.
His tongue is sharp, his eyes ablaze,
His thoughts; obscene and lack in grace.

Your eyes decline down,
You lower your head.
Your smile is a frown,
Your face's turning red.
You hear your heart bursting,
And howling for help.
But your body is thirsting,
For what lies ahead.

## I DROVE YOU BACK TO LEAVE THE WEST

I drove you back to leave the West
You pressed your face into my breast
Our parting smiles, so sad and soft
And my heart burst as I drove off

## SUN DEPRIVED PEOPLE

The sun deprived people,
Are falling down steeper.
And no one ever dares to tread,
Upon the dead that lie ahead.

And the city reeks of fear,
The antagonists draw near.
But the people laugh and cheer,
To disguise their weakened hearts,
And indulge in pompous art,
To appear mature and smart,
Until the city falls apart.

And no one ever dares to tread,
Upon the dead that lie ahead.

## RED BRICK HOUSE

The red brick house on the hill,
Stands by the well and the blue mill.
And everyday the old man plows;
The sweet, rich earth, and milks the cows.

When all is done, he laughs and grins,
And lets the wind caress his skin.
And life is easy, undismayed,
The old man sings under the shade.

Until the sun descends afar,
Surrendering to all the stars.

## ODE TO VIETNAM

The Vietnamese are peaceful people,
With spirits full of life and joy.
Their hearts so kind and smiles so gleeful,
And every little girl and boy;
Run 'round with bare feet in the streets,
With laughing faces, bright and sweet,

Then they invite me to their feast,
To offer me all that they own
And so I write this piece to thee
So your warmth won't pass unknown.

.

## LITTLE BOY

The little boy and all his peers
Are playing games in blissful cheers
When cries of joy turn into tears
And smiling faces into sneers
The sirens squeal and planes appear
And little children run in fear

Bombs are dropped all through the year
With every shower more severe
Until the city's turned to dust
And there is no one left to trust
And children's limbs are torn apart
Under the weight of purple hearts

Life goes on with new souls born
Until there's no one left to mourn
Another life, another birth
The little boy lay in the earth.

## THE LITTLE BOY IS M I A

The little boy is M I A
Presumed slain, amidst foul play
A letter's sent to mom and dad;
"Your son is dead, do not be mad".

## ODE TO A BEST FRIEND

I am not sure how to begin
I fear my wit's betraying me
But to convey the way I feel
I must insist for all to see

That even poetry at times
In perfect symmetry and rhymes
Cannot do justice to a friend
That even words cannot transcend

But at this moment, let me try
To do my best and dignify
The one, to whom I write this piece
Through these feelings, now released:

I thank you, friend, from all my heart;
The one you shaped, gently and smart.
For all you've seen
And all you've been

For every fight and every pain,
And every tear that fell in vain

For every *how*, and every *why*,
For all the times you had to cry

For everything that you have taught
And all the battles you have fought.
Without your grace, without you calm,
I know not what I would become.
A beast at best, at worst a thug,
Insecure, frightened and smug.

You filled the void the best you could
And really, who could ask for more?
And though, at times, misunderstood;
You've come out stronger than before.

As such, this piece has been to date,
The toughest thing I had to write.
But out of every rhyme I've made,
I hope this brings you most delight.

And I hope that you do laugh,
And when you cry, it is of joy,
And I hope that you do smile,
For your laughter and your bliss,

Has always calmed my worried mind.

This poem is for you, mom,
I truly tried to do it justice.

## I KNOW THE WORDS YOU WANT TO HEAR

I know the words you want to hear,
You want my whisper in your ear.
But when I do, you'll disappear,
For things are never what they seem.

## THE TRAIL OF DESOLATION

One hundred years went out of mind,
And out of sight it set.
But the torment still won't subside,
Nor can our hearts forget;
That million's lives have been denied,
And million's more upset.

Yet a nation lies and bluffs,
And blindly fails to see;
That hundred years are not enough,
Nor will a thousand be.

# MOMMY KEEPS ON CRYING

Mommy keeps on crying;
There seems to be no money.
Daddy's gone to find support,
The food supply is growing short.

The winter wind is blowing cold,
The fire in the oven glows.
Brother's sick and sister's smiling,
Every breath is growing soft.

Mommy's eyes are running;
There seems to be no money.
And daddy's back but broke,
Stomachs turn and prayers choke.

The wind is growing violent,
The fire in the oven wafts.
Brother's sick and sister's silent,
Every breath is turning soft.

Mommy grows delirious;
The food is all but gone.

Daddy's eyes are serious;
For he seems quite withdrawn.

The wind is pounding on the door,
The fire in the oven gnaws.
Brother's still, forevermore,
And there are no more breaths to draw.

## THE STAGE

The music ends, in strides Macbeth
He drinks to life awaiting death
In runs her Majesty the Queen
But does not tell of where she's been

Hamlet cries and leaves the scene,
Captain Black kneels for the Queen
The Queen embraces Mr. Beam
In marches proudly, Ho Chi Minh

He looks around in disgust
And talks of all he feels he must
Mr. Daniels' close by
He drinks martini, looking shy

Lenin looks up at the moon
And howls "the end is very soon"
The Man of Steel thanking the snow
Finds his foe in Mexico

Napoleon yells for Fouché
To write a speech full of clichés

Robespierre corrects his errors
To quickly start the Reign of Terror

Jesus preaches of remorse
Nietzsche's talking to a horse
Mr. Mojo crawls the stage
MLK waits for a change

Rosencrantz and all his friends
Hang themselves for greater ends
Godot at last reveals his face
But leaves again in loud disgrace

Mr. Blake runs on the green
Singing songs of all he's seen
Oedipus plucks out his eyes
Welcoming his self-demise

Iago takes the center stage
And locks the Queen into a cage
Othello enters in distress
And turns his wife into a mess

Mr. Shelley aids his wife

To draft the best book of her life
And life is good and full of glee
Until he drowns himself at sea

Swift employs relentless wit
Finding a solution for the Brits
Socrates dies for the truth
Despite corrupting all the youth

In an act of retribution
Martin drafts a resolution
To prevent an institution
From subtly selling absolutions

Shylock standing 'front the court
Begs the juror for support
After turning down in gold
Three times more that he is owed

Hamlet enters one last time
But forgets all of his lines
Ophelia runs to his aid
Crying that she has been made

The curtains close, the lights grow dim
All the people clap and scream.

# SHORT STORIES

# THE STING

There is a sting in your heart reminding you of the cigarette you smoked six months ago. The second sting dries your throat and pressures your memory to reveal that it was actually four and not six months ago that you smoked that cigarette. And if the third sting hits you within the next five minutes, you assure God that you will give away all of your belongings and fight world hunger if only you don't die within the next sixty seconds.

Most of the time you don't die, and to honor your vow, you give a dollar to a homeless guy. To celebrate the fact that you are alive you buy an Xbox and mass murder.

While looking for clean underwear, you stumble upon the American Spirits that you now remember were actually bought two *weeks* ago. In a moment of hesitation you remember someone saying at some party that American Spirits are "like, not bad for you at all." You buy the homeless guy a cheeseburger and light up.

There is a sting in your heart and you squash the remaining two cigarettes, throwing the packet violently into the trash, cursing Phillip Morris and that fucking idiot at the party. There is a second sting. You pack the Xbox and the twenty-two games to give away, first thing in the morning.

While cleaning your apartment with Rosetta Stone, you are struck with a third sting. Falling to your knees, you beg you heart to stop the symphony and God to forgive your broken promises, promising to never break another promise.

The next morning you buy six packets of nicotine gum, two packets of nicotine patches, and a Tony Robbins book. You volunteer diligently at the homeless shelter for three days straight, and you even shave every morning. You have not had a drink in three weeks, and you finally gave away the Xbox. You've been a good sport.

But you forgot the trash.

# CLOSE COVER BEFORE STRIKING

She looked good in the coffin. Better than ever, actually. The funeral folks had done a fine job making her look more alive than she had ever been. She had never had the slightest hint of femininity in her. For his confirmation, she had come dressed in a white t-shirt that said, ALL PRIESTS ARE PEDOPHILES, and once her fourth beloved had left her, she stopped wearing cosmetics altogether.

The funeral parlor was empty. Sitting in complete serenity, Melvin wondered why he couldn't cry. Deep down, he had to feel *something*. He knew nobody had the right to judge him for not crying, and though it felt natural to cry, he could not.

All his life, he had tried to love her. He drew her landscapes and made her gifts out of anything he could find. He wrote her poetry, and he wrote her songs and played his guitar with much skill and effort and...she proved unlovable.

Melvin's father was not around; war had demonstrated the brute nature of men leaving him in a state of chemical imbalance, and he didn't spend much time with his son but preferred the company of his long-time friends, Mr. Daniels and Mr. Beam, until the two claimed his life on his son's seventh birthday.

Melvin's scars were *mostly* physical, and by her doing. She had once poured boiling water over him for his lack of vigilance after he had gotten robbed getting her pills. He had begun boxing to blame the bruises on the sport and reassure the troubled adults that everything was all right. When he was old enough to strike her back, he did not.

Melvin hurried to the bus station after the ceremony, with her remains in hand. He was running late, threatening to ruin his perfect record of twenty-two knockouts. In his ten years as a boxer, he had never been late to a fight.

His hand dug into the right pocket of his threadbare coat and reappeared with a white matchbook he had been given at the parlor. "Think outside the box, plan your funeral-Kleinfeld & Sons Mortuary" was written in black. He flipped the matches, "CLOSE COVER BEFORE STRIKING. KEEP AWAY FROM CHILDREN."

The blue bus arrived at last, and Melvin got on. A sudden jerk of the wheels forced the urn from Melvin's grip; it fell to the floor and burst, and so did Melvin's heart as he fell to his knees, hopelessly trying to gather the remains of his mother, desperately thrusting the dust into the torn side pockets of his coat.

And then Melvin cried.

A stout toddler arched beside Melvin and stretched out the brown paper bag of his Happy Meal without uttering a word, but Melvin would not accept it. Instead, he stood up, emptied the side pockets where the remaining dust had stuck onto the cloth of his coat, and exited the bus.

He entered the ring where his opponent, a scrawny Irishman, was waiting in the corner. He began with a jab, moved his head to the left and followed with a violent uppercut. Another jab, feet swiftly to the left, right, then a hook to the ribs, and another to the head, and another one, and another one, and another one...

# I WASN'T CRYING OVER YOU

I was seven, which meant that my father had been gone for seven years. Everything is easy at seven, the summers long and brave, and everything, infinite and unperturbed. My eyes were still too young to be malevolent and my tongue too pure to cause pain.

"Come on, I really have to go." I kept jumping up and down.

"I think I've lost the key."

"Very funny."

He *had* lost the key. "He" is my older brother Charlie, and Charlie had just made us homeless. Mom was gone to bury our grandfather in the old country, and there was no spare key.

Charlie jerked the steel door as hard as he could, hoping for it to feel our despair and let us into safety, but the door proved relentless, and though I felt a stabbing pain in my stomach, I did not cry.

I was afraid of the dark, however, and though my brother pretended like he was not, I knew we shared the same anxiety. Outside, it was getting dark and my heart raced, and I looked at Charlie and asked what we should do.

After a few minutes of deep thought, Charlie concluded the best course of action was to retrace our steps. We went back to the playground where my brother had bounced around like a bunny on batteries, but it was dark, too dark to see, and there were a million scenarios in which the key was lost.

"The cops!" I yelled to my brother.

"Where?" Charlie turned around.

"Let's go to the cops! They will find mom!" I yelled again.

"Stop yelling."

"Let's go," I whispered.

My brother took me by the hand and led me back to the apartment complex.

"We'll sleep here." He pointed to the narrow space underneath the mailboxes by the entrance.

"We can't sleep here," I protested. "What if someone sees us?"

Charlie crouched below the mailboxes and pushed his body as far into the corner as he could, trying to glide into the wall.

"You can't see me, can you?" Charlie whispered, hiding his head in his palms.

"Yes, I can," I said.

"No, you can't; stop lying."

"Wait, why don't we go to the roof?" I said.

"Arch down here, before someone sees us," Charlie said, but I did not move.

"You'd rather sleep with homeless people?" Charlie went on.

"There are no homeless people on the roof! You need to know the code to get through the front door," I said.

"If you don't believe me, you can go and see for yourself," Charlie said.

"I will."

"Go ahead, but if you get stabbed by some maniac, I'm not going to save you."

The word "maniac" unsettled my already upset stomach.

"I'm going." I took my first step.

"As you wish." He wasn't buying my bluff, so I took another step and looked back.

"I'm going," I repeated.

"I know," Charlie said, still hunched below the mailboxes.

I took a couple more steps and reached the first floor.

"I told you," I shouted.

The only floors with working lights were the second and the fourth, making my heart drum faster for every anxious step I took, unsure of what it was I was trying to prove and to whom. I reached the third floor. It was dark, and there were five more stories to go.

"I'm almost there!" I shouted in fear.

My brother had not said a word, and I began trembling, and then I heard the awful sound of metal bouncing heavily against metal. *The front door!* I flew down the stairs, scratching the side of my thigh on a rusty nail that had been resting there, waiting to tear my flesh ever since we had moved for the fourth time in two years.

Charlie was gone! My knees softened and I felt sick in my entire body. I ran into the street, shouting for Charlie, but nobody answered. I heard a noise from the playground and ran towards it, but he was not there. All I saw was a homeless man digging through the trash containers, talking to someone only he could see.

At last, I cried. I was homeless and "brotherless." I went back inside the building to weep in peace and had barely reached the first floor when a sudden, hysterical laughter came from behind me.

"Charlie! Charlie! Where are you?" My brother was imitating me, unable to stand straight.

"I'm telling Mom!" I yelled, as my sobbing intensified and so did Charlie's laughter. In my distress, I was happy to reunite with my brother and finally calmed myself and dried my tears with the ragged sleeve of my dirty t-shirt and told Charlie that I hated him.

Having both calmed down, we decided to go to the police station; it was only a ten-minute walk, and though the darkness terrorized us, we found courage in being together.

ooo

"Where's your mother?" the cop began through his nose.

"Gone on business," Charlie said.

"Is there a phone you can contact her on?"

"No."

The cop inhaled deeply and rubbed his eyes for what seemed an unhealthy duration, stood up, took the Parliaments from the table and yelled, "Anton! Come here and take care of these kids," and left the station.

We sat in silence for almost an hour until Anton came in by chance, smelling the way my uncle did on weekends.

"What do you want?" the cop spotted us.

"We can't get home," Charlie said.

"Your folks kick you out?" Anton lit a cigarette.

"We lost the key," Charlie replied.

"*He* lost the key," I betrayed my brother.

The door to the station flew open and a tall, sturdy policeman with a thick beard and solemn eyes entered, dragging behind him a man who reeked of urine and could hardly stand on his feet.

"This is not a way to t-t-t-treat war heroes!" the drunkard mumbled. The solemn-eyed policeman pushed him into one of the three small cells where the prisoner repeatedly spat on the floor in protest and then proceeded to curse himself into oblivion, falling face down into his own saliva.

The tall policeman washed his hands in the sink by the cell and left the station without once looking at us. Anton looked at the prisoner in contempt, shook his head and cursed loudly and then turned his gaze back to us.

"Where are your parents?" he asked.

"Dad is dead; Mom is gone for the weekend," Charlie kept repeating.

"Any friends or relatives you could call?"

"No," Charlie said.

The cop looked at us with an expression that was a combination of pity and delight, and I thought of the time when Charlie and I stoned a mouse to death on our way to school.

"Maybe we could go to Mrs. G," my brother whispered to himself in an epiphany. The cop got up and stretched his back, moaning painfully.

"Go to Mrs. G," he said, stretching.

"What if she's not there?" I asked desperately.

"Then you're welcome to sleep with this son of a bitch." The cop smiled a disgusting smile, pointing at the sleeping veteran.

As we left the station, I turned to my brother.

"Why did you say that Dad was dead? He's not dead, he's just...gone."

"What's the difference?"

"There is a *big* difference."

"Shut up."

I did shut up. *Why was I defending him anyway?* He had betrayed me as recklessly as he had betrayed my brother, and I couldn't even remember what he smelled like.

The clock had passed twelve and it was much colder now, and we walked in silence, shivering through our thin t-shirts that we had worn forever. We reached the building where Mrs. G lived and knocked on the wooden door of her one-bedroom apartment that she rented out to a marine.

"Who is it?" Mrs. G asked through the door.

"It's us," we whispered in synch.

Mrs. G opened the door, put on her glasses that were hanging by a black chord down her heavy, wrinkled neck and squinted at us.

"What happened?"

"I lost the key, Mrs. G; we can't go home," my brother pleaded, ashamed.

"You little monkeys. Get in, get in." Mrs. G gestured and I felt the warm, reassuring smell of her home and thought of Mom.

Mrs. G didn't ask any further questions but prepared a bed for us to sleep in, which for some reason was already warm.

"Mom is coming back tomorrow," I whispered to Charlie.

"I know. Go to sleep."

I turned my back to Charlie and closed my eyes.

"I wasn't crying over you," I whispered.

"I know," Charlie whispered back.

# TERENTI

His name was Terenti Yachvilli, and he was an old, Georgian man who used to sit in solitude by the swingers holding his beautiful, handmade cane and smoke out of his wooden mouthpiece looking into nothingness.

He talked gently and in low tones, and anytime someone asked him for his name, he would carefully look up and slowly pronounce it in three parts: Te-ren-ti.

A remarkably thick pair of glasses rested on his pointy, red nose and enormous ears. He had a strong jaw, thick, white hair and kind, defeated eyes. He had been struck by a grenade in the Great War, and it rang in his ears every second of the day, every day.

Terenti lived by himself in a one-bedroom apartment in the suburb of St. Petersburg ever since his orphaned grandchildren, Alexandre and Nikolai, were deployed, and it had been weeks since Terenti had heard from them. The newspapers told of an intensified conflict, and every day, letters were sent to mothers and fathers of Russia.

Terenti sat in his usual spot, on the very edge of the bench, and smoked his Belamorkanals, which were queer-looking cigarettes (called *papirosas*). They were mostly paper and very little tobacco, had no filters and smelled terrible. He always smoked the papirosa through a wooden cigarette holder as he looked into the vacuum ahead and murmured something under his nose.

It had been a very long and warm summer, and we played ball until it got dark and our stomachs could not take it anymore. Waiting for Charlie to finish breakfast, I sat down on the bench next to Terenti, who had insisted that I call him by his first name and never say sir.

"Hi Terenti, how are you?"

"As good as the Lord permits," Terenti said, slowly turning his sunburnt face to me.

"And how good is that?" I asked.

Terenti dug into the left pocket of his thick, black coat that looked too heavy for the heat, and reappeared with a broken papirosa.

"Why don't you carry your cigarettes in the pack, Terenti?" I asked.

The old man did not respond but lit the cigarette and blew out the smoke in an all too familiar way, and I inhaled the awful smell of the cheap tobacco and moved away from Terenti so Mom wouldn't smack me thinking I had smoked.

"And why do you smoke Belamors?" I asked. "My uncle says it's the worst tobacco money can buy."

"Habit," Terenti paused, "is the great deadener." He looked at me solemnly. "Do you understand?"

"Yes." I did not understand.

"It used to be the finest tobacco," Terenti continued.

"When?" I asked.

"Before the collapse."

"How old are you, Terenti?"

"I don't remember." He grinned slowly, and I saw his toothless mouth and remained uncomfortably still.

"Did you serve in the Great War?"

"Yes," Terenti said.

"Where?" I asked.

"Leningrad."

"Were you there under the blockade as well?"

Terenti took the remains of the cigarette out of his wooden mouthpiece, put the cigarette holder in his pocket and threw the bud in the sandbox and grabbed hold of his cane with both hands.

Charlie approached the playground holding a ball with too many holes that would deflate on a regular basis, and a small, black pump to keep the ball alive every twenty minutes or so.

"Hi Terenti, how are you?" Charlie asked.

"As good as the Lord permits," I imitated the old man.

"Off to play ball?" Terenti asked.

"Yes. Do you want to come and watch?" Charlie said.

"Not today." Terenti smiled.

"Let's go. They're waiting for us," Charlie said to me, and we bid Terenti farewell and left him in his loneliness.

"He survived the blockade," I said as we approached the field.

"I know. He has a shit load of medals," Charlie said.

"How do you know?"

"Alex showed me," Charlie said.

We approached the field and shook hands with the boys, firm and friendly. I looked at Charlie as he was jumping up and down in the goal, unwillingly sacrificing himself to be the keeper, and I asked him whether he thought the brothers were coming back and he said that he did not want to think about it.

We played for hours, and when Mom came to the field to announce dinner, we said we weren't hungry, and when she asked what we had eaten besides breakfast, we lied and claimed our friends had brought sandwiches, as we continued chasing the ball through fatigue and hunger.

When it got too dark to see, we went back and I saw Terenti on the bench and wondered whether he had been sitting there the entire day.

"Hi Terenti," I said as we drew closer.

"Did you win?" the old man asked.

"Of course," Charlie said.

"That's good," Terenti said and lit a Belamore.

"Can I have one of those?" Charlie asked and looked to our balcony to see whether Mom was observing.

"Sure." Terenti handed my brother a cigarette.

"You know she will smell your fingers, don't you?" I said to Charlie in our tongue.

"That's why you do this." Charlie looked around the dark playground and found two thin branches he picked up and held like chopsticks, holding the cigarette in between the wooden pieces, never touching it with his hands.

We had learned the lesson to keep our fingers free from cigarette smell after Mom had surprised us by not only smelling our shirts, but our fingers. She had smacked us across our mouths and we struggled to fight back the tears, not because the slap was painful but because it was she who had delivered it.

"Is it true they gave you a bunch of medals, Terenti?" I asked.

Up from our balcony, we heard our mother's cry and told her we would be home soon.

"Everyone got one," Terenti said.

"What did you do?" Charlie asked, looking at our balcony before forcing the smoke on his lungs.

"Prayed to God I wouldn't die," the old man said.

"Is it true your ears are ringing all the time?" I asked Terenti, and Charlie looked at me and shook his head in disapproval of my question.

"Yes, but nobody has been answering for fifty years!" Terenti said and I saw him laugh for the first time and chuckled myself, insincerely and out of courtesy.

"What about the Blockade?" Charlie said and looked up at our balcony once again before putting the cigarette to his mouth.

Terenti's face became stern and his eyes took on a severe gaze, and he was looking into space again. We were all silent for a minute.

"Eight hundred and seventy one days of hunger," Terenti said.

"They didn't give you food? I asked.

"We lived on hundred and twenty five grams of bread," the old man said.

"Jesus Christ," Charlie said.

"Christ wasn't there," Terenti said and paused. "At first, the dead were buried with dignity and later they were buried in piles."

"Why?" I asked.

"Because even the gravediggers starved," Terenti said and lit another cigarette. "A frozen crow fell dead in the street in front of a crowd and they flew on the bird and fought each other over it. People looked like skeletons long before they died. More and more corpses lay in the streets and under the snow. And kids were orphaned by the hundreds, because mothers would give their rations to their children and starve themselves." Terenti pulled out his handkerchief and wiped his face. "And then the snow melted and revealed the corpses by the thousands."

Charlie and I stood quiet.

"Then they sent us to hold the front where I was shot," the old man said.

"Where were you shot?" Charlie asked.

"I received one right here." Terenti let go of the cane and pulled down the collar of his coat, and I saw a scar the size of a penny right above his collar bone and pictured the old man as a young soldier bleeding from his neck.

"It went right through," he said.

"Did it hurt?" Charlie asked.

"I don't remember," Terenti smiled, grabbing hold of his cane again.

Charlie plucked a few leaves of sorrel and chewed the sour plant to get rid of the tobacco taste and asked me to smell him.

"You're done," I said.

"Really?"

"Yes, chew some more," I said. "But don't pluck it here; dogs usually piss here."

"Yeah, right," Charlie said.

"They do," I said. "Even I have pissed here."

Charlie called me an animal and walked towards our house to pluck the uncontaminated sorrel. I looked at Terenti and saw he had not paid any attention to us but sat with a lifeless gaze that had become his trademark.

"Have you heard from the boys, Terenti?" I asked.

The old man sat like a statue, not moving a muscle, though I knew he must have heard me.

"Terenti?" I said.

"Yes?" The old man came alive and looked at me.

"How are the boys?"

"I don't know," Terenti said in a very low tone.

Charlie came back stuffing his mouth with more leaves than he could chew, and we looked at the old man who was no longer looking ahead but had turned his head to the side, away from us. He didn't move. Charlie looked at me uncertainly, and I shrugged my shoulders because it was too dark to see whether Terenti was crying or not.

"They'll be back, Terenti," I said. "I know it."

Charlie approached me and squeezed the back of my arm and whispered for me to stop talking.

Mom called for the second time but in a very soft voice, and we knew this was our last warning. We wished Terenti a good night, and he said we were good boys without looking at us and wished us a good night in return.

Autumn came and leaves fell, and I walked the crowded streets of St. Petersburg, and listened to the sound of wheels moving heavily against the wet asphalt and admired the way everything changed color in the rain.

Terenti had stopped coming to the playground, and I thought of Alex and Nikko and feared the worst. The old man had finally received a letter, but not from his grandsons. The department of war regretfully announced the death of Alexandre and Nikolai Yachvilli.

Terenti traveled to the front to gather the remains of his grandchildren, but the corpses had been badly mutilated, and it was impossible to say who was who.

# THE END

Dear friend, now that you finished this book, I would like to thank you yet again for taking the time to read it and I hope that you liked it.

As a last thing, would you please, please, please, leave an honest review on Amazon? Even a short review helps and it'll mean the world to me!

Add me on Instagram for more poetry and DM me your thoughts regarding the book.

My Instagram is @vincenthunanyan

Nothing makes me happier than people reaching out with their thoughts, so don't hesitate for a second and write to me! All replies come from me personally.

*Thank you, and keep smiling!*

# ABOUT THE AUTHOR

Vincent Hunanyan was born in 1991 in Armenia and grew up in St. Petersburg, Russia. His parents divorced when he was a toddler, and he was raised by a single-mother.

In 2001, Vincent moved with his family to Sweden. After graduating high school, he moved to Los Angeles at the age of 19 where he attended Santa Monica City College and later UCLA, where he received a B.A. in English with a concentration in creative writing.

*Black Book of Poems* is Vincent's first official title, and is a poetry collection dealing with loss, love, pain, happiness, depression and abandonment.

On September 21, Vincent published his second book, *I Wasn't Crying Over You,* which is his first short story collection, mainly comprised of tales derived from the author's childhood growing up in St. Petersburg and his transition from childhood to adulthood.

Vincent lives in Stockholm, Sweden, currently working on his next project.

CPSIA information can be obtained
at www.ICGtesting.com
Printed in the USA
BVHW071349121118
532888BV00011B/373/P

9 781732 597501